Frankfurt Travel Guide

Roy Writt

Table of Contents

Chapter 1

Introduction to Frankfurt

Frankfurt am Main, with a population of around 648,325, is the biggest city in the German state of Hesse and the fifth-largest city in Germany, after Berlin, Hamburg, Munich, and Cologne. There were 1,468,140 people living in the Frankfurt urban area, which is located outside of the city. The city lies at the heart of the broader Frankfurt Rhine Main region, Germany's second biggest metropolitan region with a population of 5 million.

Frankfurt is the financial and transportation hub of Germany, located on the Main river. The European Central Bank, the Frankfurt Stock Exchange, and one of the two biggest financial centers in continental Europe (the other being Paris) are all located in Frankfurt. According to Liverpool University, Frankfurt has the highest GDP per capita of any city in the European Union. It is one of nine Alpha global cities, according to the ranking.

Although Germans sometimes refer to the city by its full name to differentiate it from the other Frankfurt, known as Frankfurt (Oder), in the German state of Brandenburg, the city is more generally known simply as "Frankfurt" among English speakers. It was once known as Frankfurt am Main in English under the name Frankfort-on-the-Main.

European Central Bank, Germany

The towns and municipalities of Hattersheim am Main, Kriftel, Hofheim am Taunus, Liederbach am Taunus, Sulzbach (Taunus), Schwalbach am Taunus, and Eschborn form the Main-Taunus district, which borders Frankfurt to the west. The Wetteraukreis, which borders Frankfurt to the north and includes the towns of Karben and Bad Vilbel, forms the northeastern border.

The city is split into 118 Stadtbezirke, or city districts, which are further divided into 46 Stadtteile or Ortsteile. Sachsenhausen-Süd is the area's biggest Ortsteil. The majority of Stadtteile are integrated suburbs, Vorort, or once independent cities. Some, such as Nordend, emerged during the Gründerzeit, a period of the city's explosive expansion after the unification of Germany. Others were created from communities that had already been a part of other city divisions, notably Dornbusch (Frankfurt am Main).

The 16 area districts, or Ort Bezirke, consisting of the 46 city divisions, each have a district committee and head.

Frankfurt is a city rich in history, culture, and dining options. Additionally, it serves as Europe's financial and commercial hub. Frankfurt is more than simply a stopover location, albeit lacking the attractiveness of Munich or Berlin (Frankfurt's airport is one of the busiest international airports therefore many travelers have brief stopovers here).

As a significant city-state in the Roman Empire for more than five centuries, Frankfurt was known as the Free City of Frankfurt. The city is now very diverse, with a quarter of the population being foreign-born and half of the population having a foreign ancestry.

Frankfurt is really worth seeing for a few days, despite the fact that the majority of visitors never leave the airport. Spend the evening at one of the city's renowned cider houses, unwind in a beer garden, pass the day in a free park, or learn about the history of the area at a museum.

It's interesting to note that "Hot Dogs" and "Frankfurters" are both names for the same food, which gets its name from the city. People were allegedly given Frankfurter Würstchen during celebratory occasions like imperial coronations.

Have you heard of the Goethe Institute for language or German instruction? Goethe was a well-known author and politician in Germany who also resided in Frankfurt with his family. Anytime you're in the city, you may stop by the Goethe Haus to learn about him, wander around the home, and immerse yourself in history.

Frankfurt is frequently referred to as "Mainhattan" because of its location along the Maine River and its impressive buildings. The 55th level of the MAIN Tower, which is referred to as "Frankfurt's highest vantage point," offers an excellent perspective of the city. The Commerzbank tower, at 260 meters, is the highest.

Johannes Gutenberg, the creator of the printing press, was born in Frankfurt. On the Rossmarkt plaza in the city center, you can see a monument honoring him and the early printing press pioneers.

Frankfurt Central Station is referred to by Deutsche Bahn as the most significant station in Germany because of its central position in Germany and function as a transportation hub for both long and short distance travel. If you ever find yourself in Frankfurt Hauptbahnhof, exit the structure from the front and pay special attention to the main door. The statue of Atlas holding the Earth on his shoulders will catch your eye.

Deutsche Bahn, Frankfurt.

There is a particularly unique trip into childhood available to fans of fairy tales. The Grimm brothers resided in Hanau, about 25 kilometers from Frankfurt, and were the authors of several fairy tales, including Cinderella, Rapunzel, Snow White and the Redheaded Stepdaughter, Sleeping Beauty, and many more. Later, they relocated to Marburg, a city some 100 kilometers distant, to continue their studies.

The fourth-largest airport in Europe (and the largest in Germany) is Frankfurt Airport, where you may have had a flight connection at some time. It covers an area of 2000 hectares, has a baggage system the length of 1.5 marathons, welcomes more than 60 million people a year, manages more than 460,000 flights, and moves more than 2 million tonnes of cargo.

Chapter 2

Arriving the country

By Air

Frankfurt Airport (FRA) is the busiest airport in Germany and the ninth busiest airport in Europe. It is situated around 12 kilometers (7 miles) from the city core of Frankfurt. FRA is serviced by a number of airlines, including Lufthansa, Air France, British Airways, and KLM.

There are a lot of methods to go from Frankfurt Airport to the city center. The quickest method is to ride the SkyLine train, which takes around 10 minutes. The train operates from Terminal 1 to Terminal 2 and subsequently to the city center. Tickets cost €4.90 for a single trip or €9.80 for a day ticket.

Frankfurt Airport, Frankfurt.

You may also take the S-Bahn (subway), which runs from Terminal 1 to the city center. Tickets cost €3.60 for a single trip or €7.20 for a day ticket.

There are also a variety of bus routes that travel from the airport to the city center. Tickets cost €5 for a single trip or €11 for a day ticket. Additional advice for arriving to Frankfurt Airport via air:

~Book your flights in advance, particularly if you are going during peak season. ~ Flights to Frankfurt may be costly, so it is a good idea to book your tickets in advance to receive the cheapest price.
~If you are arriving at Frankfurt Airport, verify the status of your flight before you go.
~ Frankfurt Airport is a busy airport and delays are usual. You may check the status of your flight on the Frankfurt Airport website or on the airline's website.

~If you are using public transportation from the airport to the city center, get your tickets in advance.

~This will save you time and bother. You may buy tickets for the SkyLine rail, S-Bahn, and bus online or at the airport ticket machines.

~If you are driving to Frankfurt Airport, be sure you are acquainted with the road conditions and traffic restrictions.

~Frankfurt Airport is situated in a busy location and traffic might be heavy. You may check the road conditions and traffic rules on the Frankfurt Airport website.

By Train

Frankfurt is a significant railway station and is a stop on the high-speed rail network. There are direct trains to Frankfurt from several major cities in Germany, as well as from other countries in Europe.

The Frankfurt Central Station is situated in the centre of the city and is readily accessible by public transit.

Additional advice for traveling to Frankfurt via train:

~If you are going from another nation to Frankfurt, verify the train timetables in advance.
~Train timetables might vary based on the nation you are traveling from and the time of year.
~If you are going with a lot of baggage, it is a good idea to schedule a seat on a high-speed train.
~ High-speed trains provide more room for baggage than normal trains.
~If you are traveling with children, it is a good idea to reserve a seat in a family compartment.
~Family compartments feature greater area for children to play and roam about.

By Car

Frankfurt is well-connected by road to other major cities in Germany and Europe. The A3 highway passes through Frankfurt and links the city to Cologne, Munich, and the Netherlands. The A5 highway goes through Frankfurt and links the city to Wiesbaden, Mannheim, and Heidelberg.

There are a variety of car parks accessible near the Frankfurt Airport and in the city center. Parking charges vary based on the location and the duration of stay.

Additional advice for traveling to Frankfurt by car:

~Secure a parking spot in advance, particularly if you are visiting during peak season. ~ Parking spaces may be few in the city center, therefore it is a good idea to secure a parking place in advance.
~If you are traveling from another nation to Frankfurt, be sure you have the right documents.
~ You will need a valid passport and a driver's license to enter Germany.
~If you are travelling with a lot of stuff, it is a good idea to take a vehicle with a big boot.
~The city center of Frankfurt is busy and it might be difficult to locate parking spots for big automobiles.
~If you are driving with children, it is a good idea to carry along some activities to keep them engaged.
~The ride from the airport to the city center might take up to an hour, so it is a good idea to prepare some activities to keep the youngsters amused.

By Bus

Frankfurt is serviced by a variety of bus operators, including FlixBus, Eurolines, and RegioJet. There are direct buses to Frankfurt from several major cities in Germany, as well as from other countries in Europe

Chapter 3

Getting around Frankfurt

Because of its significant international airport, Frankfurt is often used as a point of entrance into Germany. After that, tourists scatter throughout the nation and onto more of Europe, but preferably not before seeing what Frankfurt has to offer.

Germany's financial center has transformed from a primarily business destination to one of the best cities in the country to visit. Numerous attractions may be found there, including world-class museums, prestigious book fairs, and a diverse dining and apfelwein (German apple cider) scene.

Visitors may easily move across the city via public transit, which is more convenient, affordable, and often quicker than a vehicle. The U-Bahn, S-Bahn, trams, and buses make up the transportation network. It is managed by Verkehrsgesellschaft Frankfurt (VGF), one of Germany's biggest public transportation systems, and the Rhine-Main Transport Association (RMV). The system is efficient, secure, and generally prompt, although it takes some getting used to. Utilize our detailed overview of Frankfurt's public transportation.

How to Use the U-Bahn in Frankfurt
The U-Bahn (underground) system often collaborates with the tram network and travels partially below ground. Within the city core, trains

arrive every 2 to 5 minutes. After 8 o'clock, frequency decreases to 10 to 20 minutes, and night buses take over from 1 to 4 a.m.

There are over 90 stations and nine combined U-Bahn/tram lines:

U1-U3: These lines branch off at Nordweststadt (U1; red), Bad Homburg-Gonzenheim (U2; light green), and Oberursel (U3; dark purple) as they go from the southern train station to the city's north.
U4 (Pink): This line connects eastern Enkheim with western Bockenheimer Warte by passing via the Hauptbahnhof.
The U5 (dark green) line connects the city center to northern Preungesheim through a tram and subterranean system. It and the U4 share a few subterranean stops.
U6 (Blue): This line travels eastward from Ostbahnhof (East Station) to Heerstraße in the west.
U7 (Orange): This line travels northeast from Bergen-Enkheim to Hausen in the west.
U8 (Light Purple): This route connects Frankfurt-Süd with northern Riedberg. U1-3 and it share songs.
U9 (Yellow): Uses the common U2 and U8 lines to go from Nieder-Eschbach in the north to Ginnheim in Nordweststadt. The only line that bypasses the city's core is this one.

How to Use the S-Bahn in Frankfurt
The local rail system in the city, known as the S-Bahn or Stadtbahn (city train), travels mostly above ground from the city center to the nearby suburbs and towns. The S-Bahn makes it simple to get to Frankfurt's outskirts and other towns like Mainz, Wiesbaden, and Hanau despite the area's high population.

During rush hour, the S-Bahn operates as often as every three minutes, but at night or in outlying areas, it runs every 15 to 30 minutes. For certain lines, service begins at 4 a.m., and all lines have full service from 6 a.m. until 8 p.m. At 2:00 a.m., the final S-Bahns depart Frankfurt. The S8 and S9 lines operate continuously. Access to the S-Bahn and the rest of Frankfurt's public transportation network is provided by the tickets.

S-Bahn stations are indicated with a "S" in green and white. Step onto the platform, stamp your ticket, and board the S-Bahn. On the platform, there are maps accessible, and electronic displays provide information about the upcoming arrival.

The S-Bahn in Frankfurt has 112 stations and 9 lines.

S1: Wiesbaden, Frankfurt-Höchst, Frankfurt City Tunnel, Offenbach Ost und Rödermark-Ober-Roden.
S2: Offenbach Ost, Niedernhausen, Frankfurt-Höchst, Frankfurt City Tunnel, and Dietzenbach.
S3: Langen, Darmstadt, Bad Soden, Frankfurt-West, and Frankfurt.
S4: Langen (to Darmstadt) - Frankfurt City Tunnel - Frankfurt-West.
S5: Frankfurt-West, Friedrichsdorf, Frankfurt City Tunnel, Frankfurt-Süd.
S6: Frankfurt-West, Friedberg, Frankfurt City Tunnel, Frankfurt-Süd.
S7: Frankfurt Hauptbahnhof, Groß-Gerau Dornberg, and Riedstadt-Godelau.
S8: Wiesbaden, Mainz, Frankfurt Airport, Frankfurt City Tunnel, Offenbach Ost, and Hanau.
S9: Wiesbaden, Mainz-Kastel, Frankfurt Airport, Frankfurt City Tunnel, Offenbach Ost, and Hanau are all included in route S9.

How to Use the Buses in Frankfurt

Some of the holes in Frankfurt's public transportation system are filled by buses. Although stations are closer together and buses are an excellent way to get a feel for the city, all important routes are covered by rail-based forms of transportation. In the north, between S-Bahn stations, particularly at night, buses are most helpful.

The location of bus stops is indicated with a circular sign with a green "H." In addition to regularly published regular timetables and routes, they often offer a small shelter and an electronic display that updates arrivals. Tickets may be bought directly from bus drivers or from machines at S- or U-Bahn stations. Use the machine next to the bus entry to time-stamp your ticket if it hasn't already been done.

Frankfurt's late-night buses

U-Bahns and S-Bahns have curtailed or stopped operation between the hours of 1 and 4 a.m., and night buses substitute those lines because they operate continuously. Numbers for Nachtbus lines start with "N." Tickets have the same price as daytime transportation.

Transportation tickets for Frankfurt

Travel on all modes of transportation is permitted with a regular ticket (einzelfahrt), which costs 2.75 euros (with a discount of 1.55). Zone 50, excluding the airport, covers the majority of Frankfurt.

Tickets include a timestamp and are good for two hours of travel starting now. It permits limitless transfers in a single direction. For instance, a single ticket is good for 120 minutes of travel inside the city, but you cannot go in one direction and then return in the same manner. Children under six do not need tickets, while those aged six to fourteen may ride at a discounted cost.

There are more ticket choices as well:

At peak periods, an all-day ticket (Tageskarte) is just somewhat more expensive than two single trips. Typically, the cost is 5.35 euros (3 euros off). Tickets are valid from the moment of purchase until the day's final operations. You should be aware that day tickets bought at price level 3 and valid for usage in Frankfurt (fare zone 50) do not work for travel to Frankfurt Airport.

Kurzstrecke: A ticket for a short excursion that is good for trips up to 1.2 miles (2 kilometers) away. The price is 1.85 euros.
Group Day Ticket (Group Day Ticket): This day pass costs 15.80 euros and is good for up to five persons (airport transfers are not included).

Frankfurt Card: For 23 euros, up to five tourists may travel from Frankfurt Airport or Frankfurt HBF for 24 hours, use all public transportation, and get discounts at the city's top attractions.

Week-pass or Wochenkarte: Valid for seven days straight.
In S-Bahn and tram stations, RMV stores, and through the RMV app, touch-screen ticket machines (fahrkartenautomaten) are available for the purchasing of tickets. You may use the app in English. The red "Stadtgebiet Frankfurt" button may be used to buy a basic ticket while going inside Frankfurt.

In S-Bahn and tram stations, RMV stores, and through the RMV app, touch-screen ticket machines (fahrkartenautomaten) are available for the purchasing of tickets. You may use the app in English. The red

"Stadtgebiet Frankfurt" button may be used to buy a basic ticket while going inside Frankfurt.

The English language is one of several available options on machines. Chip-and-PIN credit cards as well as euro coins and notes (up to 10 or 20 euros) are accepted at machines.

On public transportation, you must have a valid ticket, and it mostly operates on the honor system. To prove your ticket, you must say "Fahrscheine, bitte" (Ticket, please) to ticket controllers in uniform or in ordinary clothing when they want to see it. If you are found driving without a ticket, you will be fined 60 euros, and traffic cops are notoriously callous.

Chapter 4

Where to Stay

Undoubtedly, whether you're a first-time visitor or a business traveler, the City Centre is the best place to stay in Frankfurt. The Central Business District, the Central Station Quarter, and the Old Town (Altstadt) make up Frankfurt's urban center. Some of Frankfurt's top hotels are also located in the city's center.

Frankfurt City Centre, Frankfurt.

Best Hotels in the Centre of Frankfurt am Main

Best five-star hotel: Steigenberger Frankfurter Hof

Best four-star hotel: NH Collection Frankfurt City

Best three-star hotel: Motel One Frankfurt-Römer

Best cheap hotel: Hotel Hübler

Best B&B/guest house: B&B My Place

Best tourist apartments: Studio House Frankfurt

Where to Stay in Frankfurt for Sightseeing

As indicated above, the City Centre is the greatest place for visitors in Frankfurt. That is so, downtown Frankfurt is made up of several separate districts, and some of the attractions may be found in other places. These are some of the most fascinating Frankfurt districts:

Home to the ancient Frankfurter Römer, Alte Nikolaikirche, Historisches Museum Frankfurt and the Cathedral, the Zentrum-Altstadt neighborhood is Frankfurt's picturesque Old Town. Some of the top lodgings in this attractive district include the Hotel Schopenhauer Hof and the boutique Motel One Frankfurt-Römer.

A few hundred yards from the Old Town and based around the Zeil retail strip, Innenstadt is Frankfurt's primary commercial sector. This bustling business sector is home to some of the city's greatest hotels, including the Sofitel Frankfurt Opera, JW Marriott Frankfurt Hotel and Moxy Frankfurt City Center.

Bahnhofsviertel, Frankfurt's major train station sector, is perhaps the Frankfurt region with the widest lodging availability. Some notable hotels are the AMERON Frankfurt Neckarvillen Boutique and the Scandic Frankfurt Museumsufer.

Known for its numerous museums, including the Städel Museum, the Museum of World Cultures and the German Film Museum, Sachsenhausen is one of the finest neighborhoods to stay in Frankfurt for cultural enthusiasts. Some fantastic boutique alternatives in this Frankfurt district include The Blasky and Libertine Lindenberg.

The Best Areas for Tourists in Frankfurt: District by District

1. Zentrum-Altstadt: Best Location in Frankfurt for Sightseeing
Home to numerous historic sites, picturesque squares and gothic cathedrals, Zentrum-Altstadt, Frankfurt's Old Town, is also where many of the city's greatest hotels are situated.

Why is this the greatest location to stay in Frankfurt:
Best spot for a first timer.
Heart of the city.
Best area for sightseeing .
Römerberg.
Great public transit links.
Gothic architecture.
Walking distance to most attractions.
Great for leisure and business travellers.

Without a question, Zentrum-Altstadt is one of the nicest neighborhoods to stay in Frankfurt, Germany.
This district's name might be translated as "City Centre-Old Town"; needless to say, it's situated in the center region of Frankfurt.
Zentrum-Altstadt is less than a square kilometre in size, and its modern limits nearly mirror those of the walled medieval town.

This commercial and historic area is focused on the Römerberg. This "Mountain of the Romans" has been the headquarters of the Frankfurt municipal government since the 15th century. The region is home to the oldest buildings in the city, most of which had to be reconstructed after the Second World War. Today, the area is considered the hub of Frankfurt and routinely holds concerts, festivals and fairs.

A few feet away is the gothic Frankfurt Cathedral, one of the few structures in the city to survive the Second World War bombs. While its outside was for the most part saved, the inside was entirely gutted by fire and has since been reconstructed.

Other essential sites in the Altstadt are the History Museum, the Old St. Nicholas Church, and the Neue Altstadt, a picturesque neighborhood of cobblestone lanes and renovated medieval houses home to cafés and art galleries.

Zentrum is the best-connected district in Frankfurt because of its many metro and tram connections and its closeness to the Central Station.

Hotels in this region tend to have somewhat higher prices than the rest of the city, but it is well worth it for both leisure and business tourists.

2. Innenstadt: Ideal location in Frankfurt for business travelers.
Home to some of the highest buildings in Europe, Frankfurt's Financial District is a vibrant corporate and commercial sector filled with retail areas and some of the greatest hotels in the city.

Why is this the greatest location to stay in Frankfurt:
Very central location
Modern architecture
Zeil shopping street
Close to the Old Town and the Central Station

Best area for business travellers
Walking distance to most attractions
Impressive range of luxury & business hotels

Innenstadt, meaning "inner city", is a Frankfurt district situated just north of Altstadt. It . It formerly belonged to Frankfurt, the walled city.

While Altstadt is the oldest section of Frankfurt and is recognized for its medieval architecture, Innenstadt is noted for its large office buildings and contemporary skyscrapers, some of which are among the highest in Germany and Europe.

Dominating Frankfurt's skyline is the Commerzbank tower, a 56-story, 259 metres tall skyscraper erected in the early 1990s that is the city's (and Germany's) highest structure. The Main Tower (200 m), Taunusturm (170 m), and the 148-meter-tall Eurotower, which houses the European Central Bank's headquarters, are further noteworthy structures in Frankfurt's financial district.

Innenstadt, however, is significantly more than just banks and businesses. The neighborhood is also home to some prominent shopping malls and retail shops. Frankfurt's most renowned retail strip is Zeil, a bustling pedestrianised avenue containing stores, restaurants and some of the greatest hotels in Frankfurt.

Other features in the Innenstadt neighborhood include picturesque tree-lined squares such as Hauptwache and Konstablerwache, as well as the ancient Opera House and Eschenheimer Tor, a medieval watchtower and ancient city entrance.

Innenstadt is quite simple to explore on foot, and its numerous metro and tram stops enable you to commute to other districts of Frankfurt effortlessly. The Central Railway Station and the Old Town may both be reached by foot..

3. Westend & Frankfurt Messe: Best Area for Families to Stay in Frankfurt.
The Westend district in Frankfurt is a recommended place to stay for business travelers and families traveling with kids since it is home to the city's trade fair and a number of family-friendly activities.

The best place to stay in Frankfurt is here because:
good transport connections
It is the best place for trade exhibitions thanks to Messe Frankfurt.
Best area to stay in Frankfurt with children
Senckenberg Naturmuseum Palmengarten
Greater area
Large number of hotel options

Frankfurt's Westend neighborhood is located west of the city center, as its name suggests. Although the territory is divided into West End-Süd

27

and Westend-Nord for statistical purposes, people mostly perceive it as a single entity.

The Westend is often thought of being a posh neighborhood with bourgeois, wealthy residents and higher-than-average real estate prices. Westend is a section of Frankfurt's inner city districts, along with Bahnhofsviertel, Nordend, and Ostend.

The West End remained a fully low-density residential area up until the 1950s. However, after ten years, new office skyscrapers started to be built, especially near Opernplatz.

Westend, which is noticeably wealthier than the other areas, is renowned for both its abundance of family-friendly activities and its local landmarks. The Experminta ScienceCenter, which offers interactive displays about science, the Naturmuseum Senckenberg, a natural history museum with dinosaur bones, and the Palmengarten, one of Frankfurt am Main's three botanical gardens, are some of the most renowned family-friendly attractions in the area. Palmengarten is the largest inner-city green space in Frankfurt, together with the Frankfurt Botanical Garden and the Grüneburgpark.

The Goethe University Frankfurt, one of the top research universities in the world and the fourth-largest university in Germany, lies nearby. It is located in the IG Farben building, a massive modern-style construction built in 1930.

The enormous Messe Frankfurt is located on the district's western edge. The Messe Frankfurt is Europe's top trade show destination and one of

Frankfurt's economic drivers, with a busy yearly program that includes over 250 different trade events, fairs, conferences, and displays.

From the perspective of a tourist, Westend is one of Frankfurt am Main's most attractive neighborhoods. The area has a lot of charm, is quieter than other downtown areas, and is where many of Frankfurt's parks, museums, and attractions are located. More importantly, the area boasts a ton of different hotels and good transport links to Altstadt and other areas.

4. Sachsenhausen: The best district in Frankfurt for museums, regional cuisine, and nightlife is Sachsenhausen.

Sachsenhausen is one of Frankfurt's most fascinating neighborhoods, and it is situated on the south bank of the Main River.

The best place to stay in Frankfurt is here because:
Generally in the center
Local restaurants and cider taverns
Museumsufer

The area in Frankfurt where culture lovers should live
Südbahnhof
Accessible via public transportation
Numerous budget and mid-range hotels

Alt-Sachsenhausen, a neighborhood on the district's northern boundary known mostly for its cider pubs, attracts tourists and locals due to the abundance of restaurants that specialize in regional cuisine.

The Städel Museum, the German Film Museum, the Museum of Applied Arts, the Museum for Communication Frankfurt, and the Icons Museum are just a few of the fascinating museums and other cultural attractions that can be found in this expansive and relatively tranquil area of Frankfurt.

Städel Museum, Frankfurt.

The majority of these museums are located along the Main River's Museumsufer, a charming riverside promenade.

The Südbahnhof (South Train Station), which offers tram, U-Bahn, and S-Bahn services to the whole of Frankfurt as well as regional and long-distance (including high-speed ICE) connections to the rest of Germany and beyond, is located a few blocks south of Museumsufer.

Schweizer Straße, which connects Museumsufer and Südbahnhof, is a bustling commercial street with a distinctive local flavor that is home to bars, terraces, shops, and public transportation hubs. The neighborhood's western border is occupied by the Frankfurt University Hospital.

The southern portion of Sachsenhausen is made up of parklands covered in woodland and lower-density residential areas.

5. Bahnhofsviertel: The Most Affordable Neighborhood in Frankfurt

Bahnhofsviertel, which is home to Frankfurt's Central Railway Station, has the most housing options in the city.

The best place to stay in Frankfurt is here because:
Excellent location
Frankfurt Railway Central Station
Excellent connections to the public transportation
Contemporary buildings Budget eateries
Large number of hotel options
Bahnhofsvertel, which translates literally as "train station quarter" in German, is one of Frankfurt's most energetic areas.

It is located immediately to the east of Frankfurt's Hauptbahnhof, the second-busiest railway station in Germany. This massive station, which opened in 1888, offers international services to France, Belgium, and the Netherlands in addition to train links to every area of Germany.

This Frankfurt neighborhood, which is home to several well-known skyscrapers and highrises, became an extension of the city's Central Business District due to its strategic location and proximity to the Hauptbahnhof.

The Silberturm and the Galileo, as well as the Skyper on Taunusstraße and the Union Building on Wilhelm-Leuschner-Straße, are some of the most well-known skyscrapers in the area. The latter was the city's first high-rise skyscraper when it was finished in 1931.

Kaiserstraße and Taunusstraße, which run from the train station to the city center, are known as Frankfurt's red-light district. There are a lot of pornographic movies, casinos, and nightclubs in this area of the city. As

32

a result, the Bahnhofsvertel might be dangerous at night, particularly in these areas.

Having said that, the area is completely safe for tourists during the day, and as long as you use common sense, you shouldn't have any issues when there.

6. Gallusviertel: A Great Area to Stay in Frankfurt for Leisure & Business Travellers

Gallus is the best place to stay in Frankfurt-am-Main for the best price, and it's close to the Hauptbahnhof and Trade Fair.

Why is this the greatest location to stay in Frankfurt:
Fairly central location
Close to the Central Railway Station
Messe Frankfurt
Business hotels
Skyline Center
Wide choice of mid-range hotels and amazing pricing

Frankfurt's Gallus district is situated north of the Central Train Station.

The neighborhood gained its name from the historic gallows field west of the medieval city boundaries of Frankfurt. One of the city's four medieval watchtowers, the Galluswarte, is where the name of the structure comes from.

Formerly an industrial neighborhood, Gallusviertel is today one of the busiest commercial areas in the nation, due partially to the neighboring

Messe Frankfurt. Considered the biggest trade fair, convention and event organiser in the world, Messe Frankfurt is officially situated in the districts of Bockenheim and West End-Süd. Still, its range of impact may be felt in Gallus.

Gallus is home to the developing Europaviertel. This new inner-city area, centered on Europa Allee, was built on the site of Frankfurt's former main freight station. When finished, this massive urban development project will contain offices, hotels, residences, a school and social infrastructure, parks, shops and recreational facilities.

The towering Tower 185, a 200-metres high skyscraper replete with a restaurant and bar at the top, is the newest icon in this bustling district.

The neighborhood is also home to Skyline Plaza, one of Frankfurt's biggest retail malls and is particularly well-connected to the rest of the city owing to its S-Bahn (Galluswarte) and U-Bahn (Festhalle/Messe) stations. Frankfurt's Hauptbahnhof is also within walking distance from much of the neighborhood.

Gallus provides numerous lodgings, mainly mid-range and expensive hotels catering to business visitors. That is so, accommodation rates in this section tend to be substantially cheaper than those of the city core.

7. Gutleutviertel: The best neighborhood in Frankfurt am Main for young tourists

Sandwiched between the Main River and the Central Station, up-and-coming Gutleutviertel is one of the finest areas to stay in Frankfurt if you're searching for a trendy and contemporary location with pubs and restaurants.

Why is this the greatest location to stay in Frankfurt:
Fairly central location
Near Frankfurt's Central Railway Station
Good public transport links
Modern architecture
Emerging restaurant and nightlife scene
Marina Westhafen

Frankfurt's Gutleutviertel is positioned between the river and the railroad tracks leading to the Hauptbahnhof on the north bank of the Main.

This area, meaning "of the good people", acquired its name from the Gutleithof, a leprosy hospital constructed in the 13th century in what used to be agricultural ground outside Frankfurt's city walls.

The quarter was predominantly urbanised in the late 19th century as a working class and industrial region and is concentrated upon Gutleutstraße, a broad roadway that traverses the district from east to west.

Today, Gutleutviertel is mostly recognized for its contemporary residential and commercial constructions, notably near Marina Westhafen and along the river, where some of the city's best cocktail bars and restaurants can now be located.

Gutleutviertel's position near the train station and its plethora of fashionable clubs and restaurants make it one of the finest neighborhoods to stay in Frankfurt am Main for young tourists

8. Ostend: A Lovely and Economical Place to Stay

Home to the future European Central Bank headquarters and Frankfurt Zoo, Ostend is an up-and-coming neighbourhood in Frankfurt.

Why is this the greatest location to stay in Frankfurt:
Fairly central location
Near Frankfurt's East Railway Station
Good public transport links
Central European Bank and river views

Mid-range and affordable lodging in Frankfurt Frankfurt Zoo

The Ostend region is located on the north bank of the River Main, southeast of the city center.

This district of Frankfurt, which was once an industrial portside sector, has evolved into one of the trendiest and most populated parts of the city.

From a visitor's standpoint, this neighborhood is recognized for being home to Frankfurt Zoo. Founded in 1858, the second-oldest zoological park in Germany has approximately 4,500 animals of more than 510 species and is a major tourist destination.

Not far, beside the river, lies the European Central Bank headquarters. This contemporary twin-tower skyscraper was built in 2015 and gives a fantastic view of the River Main and the city's cityscape in the distance. Frankfurt Ost Station, which offers U-Bahn, S-Bahn, and Regionalbahn services, is likewise located in Ostend.

Chapter 5

Exploring Frankfurt

The Historic Sites of Frankfurt

Frankfurt's renowned historical sites include:

1. Römer
One of Frankfurt, Germany's most popular tourist destinations, is the medieval structure known as The Römer.

The Römer, which is situated across from the Old St. Nicholas Church, has been Frankfurt's municipal building (Rathaus) for more than 600 years. The Haus Römer is one of three city halls that were created in the same style in the fourteenth century.

Although the Römer is not a museum in the usual sense, the city sometimes utilizes it for a number of purposes, including a Standesamt or civil registration office. The first and second floors of the Haus Löwenstein also feature wedding rooms.

Römer, Frankfurt.

In 1985, UNESCO designated the Dom-Römer Quarter, which includes a number of historical building reconstructions on the Römerberg, as a World Heritage Site.

2. Neues Römer

Frankfurt, Germany's New Town Hall, also known as Neues Römer, is a town hall on the Main River. The second structure, which stood next to the Paulskirche and functioned as an administrative structure for Prussia and the German Empire in the 19th century, was the first structure. The municipal council currently meets at the contemporary Neue Römer building.

3. Städel Museum

One of the largest collections in the nation is housed at the Städel Museum, an art gallery. Over 3,100 paintings, 660 sculptures, over 4,600 photos, and more than 100,000 drawings and prints are housed at the Städel Art Institute and City Hall Gallery.

It is one of the bigger art museums in Germany with over 4,000 m2 of display area. The museum has a sizable collection of artwork from the early 15th century to the early 20th century, with a concentration on German-speaking artists.

Städel museum, Frankfurt.

The German art critics association, AICA, named the Städel "Museum of the Year."

4. Grüneburg Park

Frankfurt, Germany's Grüneburgpark is a city park. It was built in 1961 on the abandoned Stadtgut Grüneburg (Grüneburg Estate) and spans a length of 3.6 kilometers and an area of 57 hectares.

All year long, a variety of attractions are offered. It contains a children's train transportation facility, a petting zoo, and an adventure playground. In the summer, a large outdoor swimming pool with grassy places is constructed.

The Fürstengraben (Prince's Ditch) and the Schwanenweiher (Swan Lake) are the park's two lawns. More than 2 hectares are taken up by the numerous theme gardens.

Along with the two iconic buildings of the Grüneburgpark, the Mailänder Hochhaus and the magnificent Museum für Moderne Kunst, there is also a rose garden and a Japanese garden.

One of Frankfurt, Germany's three botanical gardens is the Palmengarten. It may be found in the West End-Süd area. 20 different varieties of trees and shrubs cover its 22 hectares.

6. Palace of Holzhausen
The aristocratic Holzhausen family erected the moated Holzhausenschlösschen (Little Holzhausen Palace) on their estate, which is today located in Frankfurt's Nordend.

Holzhausen, Frankfurt.

In 1710, Johann Hieronymus von Holzhausen restored the home to a design by Louis Remy de la Fosse. The little palace, which is one of the best examples of baroque old German architecture, has an octagonal layout.

7. Römerberg
Frankfurt, Germany has a public space called the Römerberg. It is situated in front of the Römer building complex, which has served as the home of Frankfurt's municipal government since the fifteenth century. The plaza, which is currently a well-liked tourist destination, formerly functioned as the traditional center of the medieval Altstadt (old town).

Römerberg, Frankfurt.

The Frankfurt Christmas Market, which is held outdoors throughout December, has a significant location in Römerberg. In 1933, a Nazi book burning took place there.

8. Eisener Steg
The district of Sachsenhausen is connected to the city of Frankfurt by the Eiserner Steg (Iron Footbridge), a footbridge.

A cantilever steel bridge was erected in 1911–1912 to replace the original wrought iron bridge, which was completed in 1868. It is 170 meters long, composed of riveted steel beams, and has two bridge piers.

The bridge was destroyed by the Wehrmacht in the closing stages of World War II, but it was swiftly rebuilt. In 1993, it had a comprehensive renovation.

Eisener Steg, Frankfurt.

9. Main Tower

In Frankfurt, Germany's Innenstadt district stands the 56-story, 200 m (656 ft) tall skyscraper known as The Main Tower. . The Main River was so called because it flows close. The building's total height, including the antenna spire, is 240 meters (787 feet). The tower has two open viewing areas for the public and five basement floors.

Two public works of art are shown in the building's foyer: Bill Viola's "The World of Appearances" and Stephan Huber's "Frankfurter Treppe / XX. Jahrhundert" (also known as "Frankfurt's Steps/20th century") wall mosaic.

A sky lobby is located between what seem to be two linked towers that make up the tower's framework.

10. The Old St Nicholas Church

A popular tourist destination in Frankfurt, Germany is the Old St. Nicholas Church, a medieval Lutheran church. Its German name is Alte Nikolaikirche.

It is situated next to the Römer city hall in Frankfurt's Altstadt, the city's historic center. There are 51 bells in the church, 4 of which are used for peals and 47 for carillons.

The Old St. Nicholas Church is a component of the United Protestant, Reformed, and Lutheran congregations that make up the modern Protestant Church in Hesse and Nassau.

The Old St. Nicholas Church survived mostly undamaged, despite severe damage to the nearby old city caused by the bombing of Frankfurt am Main during World War II.

11. Bethmann Park

Frankfurt am Main has a public park called Bethmannpark. On September 28, 1897, it was officially opened to the public after being planned and constructed by landscape architect Gustav Meyer (1841–1897).

From the Hotel Nassauer Hof, the park descends to the banks of the River Main, covering an area of 11 hectares. Chestnut trees (Castanea sativa), which border both sides of it, are present.

12. Museumsufer

The left bank of the Main River is home to Frankfurt am Main's long, uninterrupted urban promenade known as the Museumsufer. On a surface area of around 22,500 m2, it unites six museums and two art schools with nine exhibition spaces.

13. St. Paul's Church
Due to its service as the location of the first democratically elected parliament in 1848, St. Paul's Church (Paulskirche) is a national historic site in Germany. Paulskirche was demolished in 1886, and its replica, constructed between 1910 and 1914 in accordance with Max Littmann's ideas, took its place.

Through an organization named "Pro Paulskirche" that mostly depends on contributions from individuals, the church's reconstruction got under way in 1999. The new opening of the church took place on October 29, 2014.

Paulskirche, Frankfurt.

14. Goethehaus

The Goethe House is a museum dedicated to the writer located in Frankfurt's Innenstadt neighborhood. Johann Wolfgang von Goethe was born there.

With antique furniture and paintings, it recreates the environment in which Goethe spent his formative years. The Sorrows of Young Werther, Faust, and other well-known works of Goethe were also written there.

15. Brockhaus Fountain
Frankfurt, Germany is home to the imposing Brockhaus Fountain. Rudolf Bosselt, a sculptor, produced it in 1881, and upon retiring, he gave it to the city. It is situated in front of the St. Leonhard church and was officially opened on May 12, 1882.

The fountain is shaped like a pedestal with four ionic columns supporting a dome on which sits a warrior riding on top of two dolphins at the base, taking aim with his bow.

Behind this pedestal is a six-meter-tall column, at the summit of which is an obelisk with the date AD 1839 engraved on it.

16. Frankfurt Zoo

A zoo in Frankfurt is called the Frankfurt Zoological Garden. The zoo's more than 11 hectares are home to more than 4,500 animals from over 510 different species.

The zoo, which is the second-oldest in the nation after Berlin Zoo, was founded in 1858. It is situated east of the town, close to the Innenstadt. Neoclassicism from the 19th century is shown in the design of the gate.

17. Schiller-Denkmal

Friedrich von Schiller, a German playwright and historian, was honored with a monument in Frankfurt am Main. Reinhold Begas, who also sculpted the Bismarck monument at St. Paul's Church (Paulskirche) in 1888, was the artist behind it.

The monument was ultimately placed outside the Alte Nikolaikirche in 1883 after many debates about its placement. In 1773, while still a student at this old Stift gymnasium, Schiller laid the foundation for this church.

18. Schloss Isenburg

In Frankfurt am Main, there is a modest palace called the Schloss Isenburg. The counts of Isenburg formerly possessed it, but in 1317 they sold it to the municipal council of Frankfurt.

Helmut Heinen is one of the attorneys who now have offices in the building. A permanent exhibition about him and his wife, Martha, one of the most well-known German resistance fighters against the Nazis, has been on display since 2000.

19. St. Bartholomew's Cathedral
The Gothic St. Bartholomew's Cathedral is one of Frankfurt's oldest and most significant churches. It was built in the 14th and 15th centuries. You can visit a museum that displays artefacts from the cathedral's treasury and is housed in a medieval cloister.

The German Emperors built the Catholic Dome Saint Bartholomew during that era. The tower, which is 310 feet tall, provides a stunning view of the surroundings. The tower can be climbed from April to October. However, if you have faith in your god and are a devout Christian, it might be a positive experience for you.

20. Frankfurt's Eschenheimer Turm

Following a few streets, you will come to the Eschenheim Tower (EschenheimerTurm), a well maintained medieval stronghold, if you keep walking east along the main avenue.

The structure makes an impression with its spherical core and four domes that encircle a massive cone-shaped dome. A few green trees and a picturesque cafeteria at the base of the tower, along with the numerous small windows and the pale colors of the walls, make this historic location an absolutely irresistible choice to spend the afternoon in the middle of Downtown Frankfurt.

21. Frankfurt Hauptwache

Another noteworthy historical site that you simply cannot miss is the Hauptwache building, which is situated in the heart of the city. The building serves as the backdrop for a large square that serves as a major transportation hub in central Frankfurt and the surrounding areas.

But even with only two floors and a sizable rooftop, the building will keep you fixated on it thanks to its alluring Baroque architectural style. Because it is surrounded by so many modern structures and conveniences, this ancient building is undoubtedly a unique sight. It is also a location where you can relax with a warm cup of coffee or tea.This is due to the fact that it is now a repurposed version of a heritage cafe.

The main piazza in front of the Hauptwache building, "An Der Hauptwache," is also a highly well-liked retail area. It symbolizes the beginning of "Zeil" which is the most major retail district in Frankfurt.

22. Frankfurt Stock Exchange, Frankfurt

Set in a historic structure from the 19th century, with the Bear and the Bull sculptures in front, the 400-year old Deutsche Börse, the Frankfurt Stock Exchange, welcomes curious visitors and gives an insight into its everyday activity. You may take part in guided tours and then witness the lively trading floor of the third biggest trading exchange in the world. Being one of the most prominent sites in Frankfurt, the area is well linked with the local transit. Local taxis and buses are accessible from everywhere in the city to reach the site.

Stock Exchange, Frankfurt.

23. Liebfrauenkirche

In the 14th Century, a wealthy Frankfurt nobleman constructed a church near to the city walls. The chapel was eventually enlarged into a Gothic hall with a bell tower. During the 18th Century, the interior of the church gained beautiful rococo furnishings, and during the 19th Century, the Three Kings gateway was given a vestibule. After serious destruction in the War, the entire area was restored in 1954. A wooden roof has now replaced the Gothic original, and from the original interior, only the sculptures on the altar survive.

Liebfrauenkirche is often known as the "church of Our Lady". It was created in the thirteenth century. The cruciform floor design of the place is worth highlighting. The southern half of the Roman double church was demolished in the year of 1200 and it was rebuilt with a Gothic church.

Frankfurt's parks and gardens

Frankfurt is a city with a lot of green space. There are many parks and gardens in the city, providing a welcome respite from the hustle and bustle of the city center.

Some of the most popular parks in Frankfurt include:

Palmengarten
The Palmengarten is a botanical garden that houses a collection of over 6,000 plant species from around the world.

Botanischer Garten
The Botanischer Garten is another botanical garden in Frankfurt that houses a collection of over 13,000 plant species.

Grüneburgpark
The Grüneburgpark is a large park in the city center that is home to a variety of gardens, fountains, and sculptures.

Nizza
Nizza is a park on the banks of the Main River that is popular with locals and tourists alike.

Ostpark
The Ostpark is a large park in the eastern part of the city that is home to a variety of sports facilities, playgrounds, and a lake.

In addition to enjoying the beautiful scenery, there are a number of things to do in Frankfurt parks. Some popular activities include:

Hiking
There are a number of hiking trails in Frankfurt parks, providing a great way to get some exercise and enjoy the fresh air.

Cycling
Cycling is another popular activity in Frankfurt parks. There are a number of bike paths that wind through the parks, making it easy to explore on two wheels.

Picnicking
Picnicking is a great way to enjoy a day in the park. Pack a picnic and find a location to relax and enjoy the sights.

Playing sports
Many Frankfurt parks have sports facilities, such as soccer fields, tennis courts, and basketball courts.

Swimming:
Some Frankfurt parks have lakes or swimming pools, making them a great place to cool off on a hot day.

Relaxing
Of course, the best thing to do in Frankfurt parks is simply relax and enjoy the peace and quiet.

Frankfurt's Cultural attractions

Frankfurt is a city with a rich cultural legacy. There are numerous museums, theaters, and other cultural attractions in the city, giving something for everyone.

Some of the most prominent cultural attractions in Frankfurt include:

Frankfurt Museum of Modern Art
The Museum of Modern Art (MMK) is a museum that contains a collection of modern and contemporary art.

Städel Museum
The Städel Museum is an art museum that displays a collection of European art from the Middle Ages to the present day.

Schirn Kunsthalle
The Schirn Kunsthalle is a museum that offers temporary exhibitions of modern and contemporary art.

German Architecture Museum
The German Architecture Museum is a museum that recounts the history of architecture in Germany.

House of Photography

The House of Photography is a museum that contains a collection of images from across the globe.

Museum of Communication

The Museum of Communication is a museum that chronicles the narrative of communication from the earliest days to the present.

Zeilgalerie

The Zeilgalerie is a commercial mall that also includes a variety of art galleries and exhibition spaces.

Alte Oper

The Alte Oper is a music venue that was created in the 19th century. It is presently a famous venue for concerts, opera, and ballet events.

The Schauspiel Frankfurt is a theater that holds performances of plays, musicals, and concerts.

Frankfurt Opera

The Frankfurt Opera is an opera building that holds performances of opera, ballet, and concerts.

Frankfurt Opera.

In addition to the museums and theaters listed above, there are a number of additional cultural attractions in Frankfurt. These include:

The Frankfurt Christmas Market
The Frankfurt Christmas Market is one of the biggest and most popular Christmas marketplaces in Germany. It is hosted every year from late November to December and has over 250 vendors offering traditional Christmas food, beverages, and decorations.

Christmas market, Frankfurt.

The Frankfurt Book Fair

The Frankfurt Book Fair is the world's biggest book fair. It is held every year in October and draws over 7,000 exhibitors and over 300,000 guests from across the globe.

The Frankfurt Jazz Festival

The Frankfurt Jazz Festival is one of the oldest and most famous jazz events in Europe. It is held every year in July and includes some of the greatest names in jazz music.

The Frankfurt Auto Show
The Frankfurt Auto Show is one of the world's premier auto events. It is held every year in September and shows the newest models from major automotive manufacturers.

The Frankfurt Marathon
The Frankfurt Marathon is one of the biggest marathons in Europe. It is conducted every year in October and draws over 10,000 runners from across the globe

Frankfurt's Cuisine

Frankfurt is a city with a strong culinary culture. The city's cuisine is a combination of German, French, and Italian influences, with a few distinctive dishes of its own.

Some of the most popular Frankfurt meals include:

Frankfurter Sausage
Here in Germany, traditional food frequently (but not always) includes meat, sausages or cheese. So it shouldn't be a surprise that this list opens with a classic.

Frankfurter Sausages (or plain Frankfurter) are parboiled pork sausages. In order to hold the appellation "Frankfurter Sausages" (Frankfurter Würstchen, as we say in German), they had to be manufactured either in Frankfurt or the nearby region.

Frankfurters may be eaten cold (they are cooked and smoked at low temperatures, so they're safe to consume), but restaurants normally offer them hot. Traditionally, you would eat the sausages with bread or potato salad, but you could also get them with sauerkraut.

The majority of people like dipping their sausages in mustard, however other people prefer ketchup. Sometimes, you could also receive horseradish sauce on the side.

Frankfurter Sausages are a terrific quick dish in Frankfurt, and you'll occasionally find them at market booths. They are also an affordable main meal if you're going to a typical pub.

Äppler

Äppler is a kind of apple wine produced in the Frankfurt region. It is often served in tiny glasses and is appreciated as an aperitif or dessert wine.

Grüne Soße (Green Sauce)

Grüne Soße is a green sauce that is created of seven herbs: chives, parsley, chervil, tarragon, pimpernel, watercress, and salad burnet. It is generally served with boiled potatoes and hard-boiled eggs.

If you're seeking fantastic meals in Frankfurt and are vegetarian (or you need a meat-free day), you could try Grüne Soße.

The name Frankfurter Grüne Soße is protected, much as the name Frankfurter sausage. If you see it anywhere on a menu, you may be confident that all herbs are cultivated locally in the Frankfurt region. Most of them originate from a neighbourhood in the south of the city, where you can find numerous green fields.

Locals often pair Grüne Soße with potatoes and hard boiled eggs. Schnitzel with green sauce is a popular order at restaurants. . The sauce contrasts wonderfully with the breaded piece of beef and makes it into a little lighter meal.

Grüne Soße is also wonderful if you're seeking affordable meals in Frankfurt. The version with hard-boiled eggs is generally one of the most economical main meals you can get on a menu.

Apfelwein

Do you want to discover a must-try meal in Frankfurt?

It's Apfelwein.

This alcoholic drink is comparable to (hard) cider but not exactly the same. It has a sour aftertaste, which originates from the sort of apples used in its manufacture. In addition, all gas exits during its manufacture, so it's more akin to wine than to sparkling cider.

If you're seeking the most traditional meal in Frankfurt, this is it. Locals are wild over Apfelwein, and if you come in summer, you may even be able to attend an Apfelwein festival.

The finest site to sample the drink is in Sachsenhausen, a suburb on the southern bank of the River Main. Here, you may discover several classic Apfelwein bars.

You order Apfelwein in a Bembel, a grey-blue pottery jug. Make careful to indicate how many servings you want when making your purchase, since some of the Bembels may store a lot of liquid! Be mindful of the glassware's design while serving the beverage. They are called "Geripptes", and it's what you usually drink Apfelwein from.

Handkäs mit Musik
When eating the native Frankfurt food, you'll sooner or later come across Handkäs' mit Musik.

Known for more than 200 years, handkäse is a regional sour milk cheese. It's so popular in this area that in the Frankfurt Christmas market, you can even get Handkäse fondue or raclette.

Handkäs' mit Musik is not only the cheese, however. This cheese dish is called "hand cheese with music" and is made of cheese that has been marinated in vinegar, oil, caraway, salt, and pepper.. On top, you'll discover cubes of raw onion, and some say that the "music" alludes to the sound you'll make while digesting those onions.

On many menus of traditional German restaurants in Frankfurt, you may get Handkäs mit Musik as an appetizer.

Rindswurst

If you visit a market in Frankfurt (we suggest the Kleinmarkthalle as one of the greatest locations to see in Frankfurt), you will undoubtedly find someone selling grilled sausages. Besides the typical Bratwurst, which you can purchase all around Germany, you could see several darker sausages on the grill.

This particular beef sausage, known as a Frankfurter Rindswurst, came into existence in this city in 1894. Gref Volsing, a local butcher, devised the recipe for the expanding Jewish community.

Rindswurst is amongst the greatest German cuisine in Frankfurt that you can obtain. It tastes stronger than conventional sausages, and if you pay careful attention, you could catch a tinge of smoky paprika.

In order to make Rindswurst simpler to eat on the street, most vendors in Frankfurt offer it in a bread roll.You may then add ketchup and mustard to your preference.

Frankfurter Kranz

Did you know that one of Frankfurt's most well-known dishes is a dessert?

The Frankfurter Kranz fills that need for sweets among the locals. Some claim that the ring-shaped sponge cake serves as a reminder of the time when Frankfurt served as the Holy Roman Emperors' coronation city.

The cake has virtually a golden color thanks to the brittle and cherries on top, which stand in for the crown's rubies.

Buttercream is found between the layers of sponge cake. In order to balance the sweetness with a somewhat more acidic flavor, some bakers additionally use fruit jelly.
Frankfurt Crown Cake is among the greatest foods in Frankfurt, despite being quite thick and rich. It is available at a few select bakeries and cafés, mostly in the old town, and we strongly urge you to taste it.

Sachsenhäuser Schneegestöber

Have you ever noticed how Frankfurt's traditional cuisine often includes cheese or sausage? This list continues with the dish after that.

Despite having nothing to do with snow or ice, its name, which translates to "snow flurry from Sachsenhausen," is nonetheless appropriate.

With a pretzel or a piece of dark bread, you may enjoy Sachsenhäuser Schneegestöber, a cheese platter, as an appetizer. It comprises camembert and cream cheese, which combine to form a creamy and smooth mixture. While some people season their "snow flurry" with salt and pepper, others just add spices like paprika, which may make it orange.

Although spring onions may be used in place of raw onions, the combination often incorporates raw onions.

Frankfurter Rippchen

Another major dish follows in this list of Frankfurt foods. Frankfurter Rippchen is an alternative if you're unsure of what to order during your visit since we haven't introduced many of them yet.

Pork cutlets known as Frankfurter Rippchen are cured. You'll notice the similarities if you've ever eaten Kassler, another typical German meal. Frankfurter Rippchen, however, have a milder flavor since they are merely cured, not smoked.

The pork cutlets are often heated in broth or sauerkraut before being served with mashed potatoes, sauerkraut, and mustard.

The Rippchen is available at several Frankfurt restaurants that specialize in German cuisine. The majority of Apfelwein taverns in Sachsenhausen have them on their menus, making it a wonderful spot to experience them.

Bethmännchen

The second item in our list of Frankfurt's top German restaurants is a little odd, and depending on the time of year, you may not be able to locate it.

Bethmännchen are holiday sweets made with almonds.
Three almonds are used to garnish the biscuits, which have a marzipan-like dough. According to lore, they were formerly baked by a neighborhood baker for a family living in Frankfurt. One almond for each of the family's four sons, he wore.

After one of the boys passed away after a year, he stopped decorating the cookies with anything other than three almonds.

Purchasing Bethmännchen at the Frankfurt Christmas market is the simplest way to sample them. As of mid-November, you may now get them at bakeries. Due to their seasonality, they are not the most convenient dish to consume in Frankfurt, but they are definitely worth looking for.

Mispelchen
Another beverage is the last item on our list of typical Frankfurt foods.

Even though I had spent most of my childhood in Germany, I had never heard of mispelchen before relocating to Frankfurt since it is such a local beverage. It contains Calvados, an apple brandy, and a "Mispel" fruit.

Fun fact: In Germany, a fruit known as Mispel—medlar in English—can sometimes be seen in stores throughout the winter. On the other hand, the Mispel in the Mispelchen is a Japanese loquat.

When a group of friends visits an apfelwein tavern, mispelchen are fairly common. But be cautious. Although the fruit may taste sweet, it has been submerged in alcohol for some time. Overeating will cause you to get inebriated extremely rapidly.

Rindsrouladen

A beef roll called a rindsrouladen has bacon, onions, pickles, and spices within. They are often served with potatoes and cabbage and cooked in broth or wine.

Rindsrouladen

Restaurants in Frankfurt

You may be wondering where to eat Frankfurt-style foods now that you've been exposed to them.

Sachsenhausen is one of the greatest areas in Frankfurt to get a typical German restaurant. Frankfurt cuisine is available here at one of the numerous Apfelwein bars. The most of the meals we discussed will be served to you, with the exception of the Frankfurter Kranz and Bethmännchen.

Visit a classic coffeehouse or the Christmas market for them.

Unfortunately, it's hard for us to choose just one greatest restaurant in Frankfurt, as much as we would want to. The well-known Apfelwein bar Zum Gemalten Haus is well-known for both its architecture and interior decor. Ebbelwoi Unser, one of the first eateries we went to in Frankfurt, also offers excellent traditional cuisine.

If you want to dine in a garden setting while in Frankfurt, Daheim Im Lorsbacher Tal is fantastic. On a pergola, wine grows, so you always have adequate cover. The cuisine is excellent, and they mostly employ local ingredients.

The most distinctive restaurant we've ever been to is Haus Wertheym in the city center. Due to its proximity to the old town, it attracts a lot of tourists, yet Frankfurt's decorating is distinctive.

However, if you want to avoid the crowds of visitors, we suggest Apfelwein Solzer. Although most tourists don't make it here, it is quite popular with the residents and located far away from the city center.

Joining a culinary tour in Frankfurt is another excellent opportunity to sample local cuisine.

In Frankfurt, there are several excellent restaurants serving both foreign and traditional German cuisine. Here are some recommendations:

Gut Stubb
Gut Stubb is a traditional German restaurant that serves a wide variety of German dishes, including Frankfurter Würstchen, Handkäs mit Musik und Grüne Soße.

Ebbelwoi-Stube Alt-Frankfurt
Ebbelwoi-Stube Alt-Frankfurt is a traditional Frankfurt restaurant that specializes in Äppler. They also serve a variety of other German dishes.

Da Gino

Da Gino is an Italian restaurant that serves a variety of classic Italian dishes, such as pasta, pizza, and risotto.

La Maison du Boeuf

La Maison du Boeuf is a French restaurant that serves a variety of classic French dishes, such as steak frites, coq au vin, and cassoulet.

The Barn

The Barn is a vegetarian restaurant that serves a variety of creative and delicious vegetarian dishes.

Frankfurt Food Markets

Frankfurt is also home to a number of food markets, where you can find fresh produce, meats, cheeses, and prepared foods from all over the world. Here are a few suggestions:

Flohmarkt am Main

Flohmarkt am Main is a flea market that is held every Sunday in the Osthafen district of Frankfurt. It is a great place to find antiques, collectibles, and vintage clothing.
[Image of Flohmarkt am Main]

Kleinmarkthalle

Kleinmarkthalle is a covered market that is located in the heart of Frankfurt. It is a great place to find fresh produce, meats, cheeses, and prepared foods from all over the world.
[Image of Kleinmarkthalle]

Viktualienmarkt

Viktualienmarkt is a large farmers' market that is located in Munich, Germany. It is a great place to find fresh produce, meats, cheeses, and prepared foods from all over the world.

Chapter 6

Nightlife in Frankfurt

The varied nightlife in Frankfurt includes everything from upscale wine bars to jazz dancing to techno clubs. Since each of the city's neighborhoods has its own character, choosing a hub based on your plans for the evening is simple.

Bockenheim: Frankfurt is home to roughly 40,000 students, many of whom reside on the east side of the area surrounding the university.

Bahnhofsviertel: Frankfurt's red light district is known as the Bahnhofsviertel, which is the neighborhood around the Hauptbahnhof (major railway station). Although it was formerly fairly dirty, it is now attractive and boasts a large variety of bars, especially in the Kaiserstrasse area.

Bornheim: This region is home to several posh bars, particularly those along Berger Straße.

Salzhaus: Cocktail bars and those who like them thrive in this area of the city.

Sachsenhausen: This historic district south of the river is a haven for pubs and ebbelwoi (apple wine) taverns, which are a local favorite. While farther south is more suited for a laid-back audience, areas closer to the river are often more touristic, less expensive, and packed with students.

Bars in Frankfurt

Frankfurt bars might be classy, casual, or everything in between.

Club Voltaire: Club Voltaire is a shelter for the musician and activist population. It was founded in 1962 and is a beatnik bar. Daily readings, additional timely events, bar cuisine, beer, and cider are available. Expect jazz and sound tracks, as well as a relaxed atmosphere.

Dauth-Schneider: Spend some time with the locals at this apfelwein (apple cider) pub, which has been operating for more than 150 years, and work on your ebbelwoi pronunciation.

Luna Bar: The greatest cocktail bar in the city's core is Luna Bar, where you can unwind with a drink after a hard day at work or at a conference. There is live music on Mondays and DJs on the other days of the week, and the décor is just as fashionable as the beverages.

Jimmy's bar: Since 1951, Jimmy's Bar has offered genuine piano bar atmospheres in the United States. Expect a professional clientele and premium refreshments, snacks, and services.

Naïv: Craft beer has been popularized in Germany, and this is the greatest location in Frankfurt to sample more than 100 different beers from across the globe, including a number of locally created selections.

Frankfurt Art Bar: The lively Frankfurt Art Bar hosts readings, cabaret, and jazz events on a regular basis. Local and international DJs provide a cozy club environment on Fridays.

After-Work-Shipping: This after-hours cruise on the Main River explores various aspects of the city's architecture while also putting an emphasis on the ambiance via beverages and mingling.

Frankfurt clubs

While Berlin now receives the most of the limelight for Germany's iconic club scene, Frankfurt really set the bar with its internationally recognized scene.

There are lots of alternative places to dance despite the Cocoon Club being closed.

Robert Johnson: One of the top techno clubs in the world, according to Robert Johnson, is located on the banks of the Main River. Here, the tech house subgenre was created, and renowned DJs routinely perform while using their top-notch sound system. There is a stringent door policy at this venue for techno enthusiasts because of its limited capacity of 100 people.

Tanzhaus West: This underground club, housed in a former factory, features music ranging from goa trance to cyberhouse to hip-hop. In the summer, live performances and DJ sets may be seen in the outside garden.

025 Club: Originally a fire bunker, this gloomy, smokey venue plays a wide variety of music and draws young people.

Club Anthrazit features both a DJ and a VJ (Video Jockey), who project images in the appropriate colors, patterns, and forms to match the music.

The daily themes of Sachsenhausen's Dreikönigskeller, which opened in 1988, include jazz and blues, music from the 1960s and 1970s, R&B and soul, New Wave, and more.

The Cave Club is a noisy, laid-back, subterranean nightclub that plays heavy metal and alternative music.

Club Travolta is a chic, two-story club with a minimalist interior featuring hip-hop and techno music.

U 60311: For the youthful and enthusiastic, this electronic club offers over 10,000 square feet of dancing area. It was renovated in 2006 and is nonetheless grungy and entertaining despite being located in an old pedestrian tunnel.

Silbergold: This mega-club often has a big queue outside, but once inside, you may dance the night away to the music of the many different guest DJs.

The biggest club playing Latin music in Frankfurt is called Chango Latin Palace. Before club-goers samba into the night, a dance instructor gives instruction.

Final Destination Club: If you're looking for anything extreme, gothic, or heavy metal, go over to Final Destination.

Live Music in Frankfurt

Additionally, there are several jazz-focused live music venues in Frankfurt. Because of all the jazz clubs that are situated on Kleine Bockenheimer Strasse, the street is often referred to as "Jazzgasse." However, there are many locations where you may hear live music of different kinds.

Jazzkeller: Frankfurt's Jazzkeller is unquestionably the city's premier jazz venue. Here, legends including Dizzy Gillespie, Louis Armstrong, and Chet Baker have performed.

Jazzlokal Mampf: A renowned jazz venue that opened in 1972, Jazzlokal Mampf hosts more than 150 performances each year.

Batschkapp: The Red Hot Chili Peppers, The Pogues, and many more artists have performed at this alternative club since it first opened its doors in 1976.

Elfer Music Club: One of Germany's most well-known rock clubs, Elfer is a great place to hear rock, metal, and independent music.

Clubkeller: This underground venue features both domestic and foreign musicians playing indie and alternative music.

Brotfabrik: The Brotfabrik is a venue with two stages, an event space, two restaurants, and a bar that is housed within a former bakery. You may attend concerts by anything from classical musicians to independent acts.

Das Bett: Committed to setting itself apart from the crowd, all of the music performed here is from the alternative scene. Sundays are designated as "bed rest" days.

The Cave: This is the place to go if you want to party hard too loud, live music. It is known as Frankfurt's "worst-lit" club.

The daily performances at Spritzehaus, located in the heart of the cider area, will have your head bopping.

Outdoor bars in Frankfurt

The celebration shifts outdoors throughout the summer. There are several great Strandbars (beach bars) in nearby Offenbach, but here are a handful in Frankfurt that are worth visiting.

The terrace along the river is one of the greatest spots to enjoy a beverage and the scenery. Pick from a variety of tapas, beers, or wines in addition to their extensive cocktail and beverage menu.

Mantis Roofgarden: This club has three club rooms where you may dance from twilight till morning in addition to a roof terrace with breathtaking views.

City Beach Club: Sand and palm trees at this beach club make it easy to forget that you're in the middle of a big metropolis.

Chapter 7

Shopping and Souvenirs in Frankfurt

You may enjoy a world-class shopping experience in Frankfurt, the financial and economic hub of Germany. Even though it is one of the smaller major metropolises in the globe, it is home to several stunning skyscrapers, commercial buildings, and the third-largest airport in Europe. People often go there to see the outstanding art, renowned museums, and vibrant districts. You must, however, go shopping in Frankfurt whether you are a repeat visitor or a first-time visitor for business or pleasure.

The heart of the city is home to numerous well-known retail districts with lucrative shopping avenues and expansive malls showcasing top German brands. While there are many luxury brands lined up along the major shopping avenues, don't miss the opportunity to explore the confined spaces and cobblestone lanes where undiscovered treasures are just waiting to be discovered. Additionally, there are farmer's markets and flea markets where you may buy local specialities, fresh food, and other goods.

In the fifth-largest city in Germany, there are no restrictions on what you may purchase. Therefore, lay aside some money to maximize your pleasure. Additionally, you may store your baggage and shopping bags in a luggage locker in Frankfurt. In this manner, you may travel more freely across the city.

Frankfurt's top shopping streets and neighborhoods

Le Zeil

The Zeil, a bustling road that was previously the focal point of a significant cattle traffic in Frankfurt, is a genuine shopper's paradise. With its abundance of specialized businesses, department stores, upscale boutiques, and large shopping malls, it has long been one of the nation's favorite shopping regions. This shopping promenade offers everything you need, whether you're looking for new jewelry to complement your outfit, footwear, or technology.

Zeil has a history that dates back to the fourteenth century. However, this road did not discover its modern identity and was called a commercial district until the 1800s. Since then, it has grown to be one of Germany's most known shopping destinations for high-street clothing, locally manufactured gifts, and souvenirs.

Enter MyZeil Center, one of the street's largest retail centers. Zeilgalerie, a ten-floor building that debuted in September 1992, is also located there. Its stunning architecture and distinctive design are easily identifiable.

The Zeil commercial district is situated in the heart of Frankfurt. By using the subterranean train system at either end, you can get there. The

Frankfurt Stock Exchange and the Museum of Modern Art are also nearby.

Berger Avenue

Frankfurt's longest shopping thoroughfare, Berger thoroughfare (Berger Strasse), is home to a large number of independently owned stores. A welcome change from the same-old chain shops. With a flea market twice a week where you may meet actual farmers selling regional goods, it grows livelier and more lively. Additionally, it's a great place for locals and tourists to enjoy both foreign cuisine and regional specialties.

If you want to unwind or spend time with friends over drinks, the bottom half of the street has charming shops, cafés, and pubs. After an arduous day of leisurely shopping, Upper Berger Street is a great location to unwind with its classic cafés and pubs. To take advantage of the pleasant summer weather, they provide outside sitting.

Sachsenhausen

The Sachsenhausen is a charming retail district that caters to younger customers and is tucked away south of the River Main. The Schweizer Straße and the Museum Mile are its two distinct sections, and both are renowned for their quaintness and old-world appeal.

However, if shopping in Frankfurt is what you came for in the end, you should check out the area's major thoroughfare, Schweizer Straße. In comparison to Zeil, it has a slower pace and a more relaxed attitude. It is full of booksellers, fashion boutiques, delis, and stylish cafés. Along the river's banks, it blends delicious food with contemporary fashion.

The most well-liked flea market in Frankfurt is also located in Sachsenhausen. It's a great place to look for one-of-a-kind items, presents, accessories, and sampling of regional cuisine. Additionally, there are antique things, used clothes, and used furniture available. The Flohmarkt Sachsenhausen is open from 9 AM to 2 PM on the second Saturday of each month. On a Saturday morning, it's essential to come early to increase your chances of finding items that are worthwhile to buy.

Goethestraße

Goethe Street is one of Frankfurt's greatest retail districts if you want high-end luxury shopping. The majority of the most prestigious luxury and designer brands, including Gucci, Hugo Boss, Chanel, Armani, Bulgari, Louis Vuitton, Montblanc, Hermes, Versace, Prada, and many more, are centered here. It has various restaurants and cafés in addition to independent concept businesses, local boutiques, and well-known jewelry and apparel labels like Cartier and Tiffany & Co. Within a few short steps, every attentive shopper may find everything here.

The third busiest retail street in Germany is Goethestraße, one of the city's top shopping districts. It is also known as Luxusgasse, which is German for "luxury lane," or Fifth Avenue of Frankfurt. There are about 300 meters of tempting temptations along the three-lined boulevard.

Johann Wolfgang von Goethe, a renowned German author and politician, is honored by the street's name. Goethestraße, built between 1892 and 1894, has weathered the troubled history of the nation. Today, it is home to some of the most prestigious labels and most well-known businesses in the world, housed in a mix of modernist, contemporary, and historic structures.

The Kaiser Street

Frankfurt's Kaiser Street is lined with old homes from the 18th century, making a stroll down it seem like traveling back in time. In terms of architecture, it's one of the city's last intact avenues and one of the few places in Germany where tourists can still see genuine 18th-century structures that survived World War 2.

The section of Kaiser Street that leads to the main railway station in Frankfurt is renowned for its vibrant nightlife. The opposite end, however, which goes to the city center, still displays the fame and luxury of the long-gone age. Additionally, there are multipurpose shopping centers, boutiques, jewelry stores, sidewalk cafés, and restaurants there.

Boulevard Grosse Bockenheim

Grosse Bockenheimer Strasse is one of the areas worth investigating if you're going to be in Frankfurt. If you wish to browse the premium designer brands, it features a sizable pedestrian zone between Opera Square and Stock Exchange Street that runs parallel to Goethe Street. Since it combines retail centers, restaurants, and bars, there are some interesting finds here. Till you locate what you are hunting for, take your time walking along the street.

Grosse Bockenheimer street is a wonderful place to eat in addition to shopping. There are grocery stores, butcher shops, bakeries, and cafés where you may meet a friend.

Töngesgasse

Parallel to the more well-known retail road, Zeil, is another Old Town shopping route called Töngesgasse. It is home to several independently owned specialized stores, some of which have been in business for more than a century. The W.Wächtershäuser, a historic specialty store that will mark its 200th anniversary in 2022, is a prime example. The local Hensler optical store opened in 1864, while the Gambler leather shop opened its doors in 1877.

The roadway was first mentioned in 1236. Antonitergasse was at that time the most important street. It was the busiest and most lucrative commerce route in Frankfurt. The name changed as a result of linguistic developments to become what is today called Töngesgasse. Locals and businesses pay attention to the region's history. They have a street celebration known as the Antoniterfest every August.

Best Frankfurt Shopping Malls and Centers

MyZeil Outlet Center

One of the largest retail malls in Frankfurt, MyZeil retail Mall has an area of about 77,000 square meters. In 2009, it was formally inaugurated. Since then, residents and tourists have frequented there for recreation and pleasure. The architecture of the building, which has striking curved glass facades and metal panels as part of its extraordinary design, is what makes it more intriguing.

The eighth level of MyZeil Shopping Mall is home to a large number of shops. Numerous well-known national and international companies, including Bershka, Ecco, Hollister, Abercrombie & Fitch, Saturn, and others, call it home.

Enjoy a leisurely stroll around the stores while you take in the breathtaking view of the city skyline made possible by the building's translucent exterior. It has a nice ambiance, is bright and translucent, and is ideal for a day of relaxation. Take a wander outside the building if you've seen enough of the inside since there are other stores and a gallery outside.

Location: Frankfurt am Main, Germany, 60313 Zeil 106

Nordwestzentrum

At Nordwestzentrum, one of Germany's biggest and busiest retail centers, you may indulge in a leisurely shopping spree. It is situated northwest of the city, with a leasable area of about 94,500 square meters, and has over 170 retail stores, including both national and international chains.

Although there isn't much here for upscale shopping, it provides all you need for a decent living. The Nordwestzentrum is home to some great stores, including Muller, H&M, Zara, Peek & Cloppenburg, Calzedonia, and Vero Moda. There are several coffee shops, restaurants, and diners in the food court and all across the mall if you're here to eat.

Numerous public amenities are available at Nordwestzentrum, including family-friendly services, healthcare, and a gym. Additionally, visiting the mall won't be a burden since it includes more than 3,500 parking spots, as well as a central bus station and metro stations.

Area code: 60439 Frankfurt am Main, Limescorso 8

Horizon Plaza

2013 saw the formal opening of Skyline Plaza, which has only been around for a few years. With more than 170 retail stores and brands, this new mall has a floor area of over 38,000 square meters. It is conveniently situated in the city's European District, a brand-new neighborhood near to the downtown area. This makes it the ideal place to go shopping while seeing the world-class sites in and around Frankfurt.

The building's appearance and amazing architecture will wow you. But once you enter, you'll find a whole different retail and leisure experience. Every shopper must make a stop at the roof garden on the structure's roof. The fact that it provides a free viewing platform for everyone is one of the striking elements of the mall.

The building complex also includes an adjoining parking garage and the MeridianSpa fitness facility in addition to the main commercial mall. Following your shopping, you may check out the renowned food court in the center of Skyline Plaza, where you can look through a variety of eateries.

Location: 60327 Frankfurt am Main, Germany, Europa-Allee 6

Hessen-Center

Frankfurt's Hessen Center has been in operation for more than 50 years and is still one of the most popular shopping centers in the area. The Hessen Center can stay up with the economy despite having less store space than other malls in the area and is very active in the local community.

Over 115 stores selling a wide range of goods, including clothing, accessories, gadgets, and food, can be found at this mall. Additionally, it is ideally situated at Borsigallee, next to Volkshaus Enkheim and Imam Abu Hanifa - Afghanischer Kulturverein. Except on Sundays, Hessen Center is available to guests from 8:30 AM to 8:00 PM every day.

Location: 60388 Frankfurt am Main, Germany, Borsigallee 26
Whether you're visiting Frankfurt for business or for a brief holiday, don't forget to include shopping on your schedule. When considering a little retail therapy in Central Europe, it may not be the first destination that comes to mind. But it merits a place on the "must-visit" lists of all fashionistas and shopaholics. It offers everything to suit your requirements and style, from huge shopping malls and department stores to handicraft stores, small retail outlets, and boutiques.

Chapter 8

A 3 days itinerary

Things to See and Do in Frankfurt

1. Cross the Eiserner Steg
Otherwise known as the Iron Bridge, this Neo-Gothic pedestrian bridge
links the city center to the Sachsenhausen area. Built in 1869, the bridge
affords spectacular views of the city from above the Main River from
which the city receives its full name, Frankfurt am Main (Frankfurt on
the Main). Over 10,000 people cross the bridge everyday!

2. Eat and drink in Sachsenhausen
South of the Main River, Sachsenhausen features several of the top cider
taverns and pubs in the city. After visiting various bars, take a walk along
the Main River and enjoy the scenery. Sachsenhausen is also notable for
Museumsufer, a series of 38 museums along the river with themes
including the arts, architecture, and Jewish history. With the two-day
Museumsufer Pass, you may visit all the museums for only 21 EUR.

3. Spend the day in the Palmengarten
Spanning 54 acres, Frankfurt's botanical garden is the biggest of its type
in Germany. Opened to the public in 1871, the garden was visited by the
famed cowboy Buffalo Bill in 1890. Don't miss the Palm Garden with its
large variety of native, tropical, and subtropical plant life. Moreover, the
gardens also provide tons of events year-round, including concerts and
guided tours. It's 7 EUR to visit.

4. Walk about the Bornheim

The Bornheim area includes several lovely medieval-style mansions that survived World War II. Since so much of the city was destroyed in the conflict, here is your last opportunity to view what the city looked like before everything was destroyed. The city's longest street, Berger Strasse, is Bornheim's economic heart, and it's stuffed full of restaurants, wine bars, boutique stores, and pubs.

5. Stroll around the Frankfurt Book Fair

Held in the middle of October for over 500 years, this fair is considered the greatest event in the publishing sector. Publishers, authors, and creative workers from all around the globe gather to have debates, network, and celebrate the written word. It's a week-long event, but it's only available to the public for the final two days. A day pass is 25 EUR.

6. Climb the Main Tower

The most satisfying views over Frankfurt are from the top of the 56-story Main Tower, the only high-rise that's available to the public. Named after the Main River, from here visitors may ride the elevator up to an observation deck overlooking Frankfurt's cityscape. Tickets to the viewing deck are 9 EUR.

7. Visit Goethe House

Born in Frankfurt in 1749, Johann Wolfgang von Goethe is regarded as Germany's most famous writer. Born in 1749, he was a poet, dramatist, writer, and theatrical director. Destroyed during World War II, the Goethe House was rebuilt with its original furniture, paintings, and literature that belonged to the family. You may also see his writing desk, where he penned his most renowned piece, The Sorrows of Young Werther in 1774. Admission is 10 EUR and combo tickets that include special exhibits are 13 EUR.

8. Visit Senckenberg Museum

The Senckenberg Museum is a rich mine of natural history relics, featuring everything from fossils to Egyptian mummies to dinosaur bones. It's the second-largest nature museum in the nation, home to approximately 17,000 bones. One of the most astounding objects here is a fossil with a portion of preserved scaly skin connected to it. Admission is 12 EUR.

9. Check out the DialogMuseum

The DialogMuseum is certainly one of the most unusual museums in Germany. Rather than visiting a museum to examine exhibits, this museum encourages you to navigate the world as a blind or visually impaired person. On a one-hour tour of four entirely pitch-black chambers, guests experience what it's like to live without any visual signals, depending on other senses to get them through. Admission is 16 EUR.

10. Explore the Deutsches Filmmuseum

This is another unusual museum in Frankfurt, concentrating on cinema in Germany. There include exhibitions on the history of cinema, behind-the-scenes insights into filmmaking, interactive displays, film artifacts like drawings, and more. A combined admission to both the permanent and temporary exhibitions is 12 EUR. You may also view a film in the museum's theater for 8 EUR.

11. Check out the Kleinmarkthalle

If you're searching for a unique culinary experience, go over to the Kleinmarkthalle for a vast choice of high-quality fresh produce, delicatessen items and wine, handcrafted German regional specialties, and also international favorites. There are many little restaurants offering seafood, Italian delicacies, and much more. It's a nice area to roam about, particularly on a wet day.

12. See the Dom

Frankfurt's greatest attraction, its reddish sandstone cathedral, goes back to the 14th century when it was used to crown the rulers of the Holy Roman Empire. It includes a 95-meter-tall (311 feet) Gothic tower, which you may climbvia 328 steps. Admission is free, but the tower cost 3 EUR.

13. Visit the Städel-Museum

The Städel Museum features an amazing collection of art, with a major concentration on German and Renaissance art. There are nearly 3,000 paintings, 4,000 photos, 600 sculptures, and 10,000 drawings by the likes of Monet, Picasso, Bacon, Ernst Ludwig Kirchner, and others. Admission is 16 EUR.

14. Explore Römerberg

The historical heart of Frankfurt is home to magnificent half-timbered structures and some medieval buildings that date back to the 14th and 15th centuries. Most buildings were destroyed during World War II, although many have been rebuilt to depict what they used to look like. It's a wonderful area to wander and take in the local pace of life.

15. Relax in Frankfurt City Forest

The city forest is the biggest woodland located inside any city borders in Germany. The six playgrounds and nine ponds make the woodland a popular spot for individuals wishing to unwind in nature. There is also a 450-kilometer-long (279 miles) network of paths for hikers, walkers, bikers, and runners!

16. Visit Offenbach

Offenbach is a little nearby city with dozens of modest shops, a flea market, a farmer's market, an ancient baroque castle, and the gorgeous Neo-baroque Büsing Palace. Offenbach is the ideal destination to escape the bustling metropolis for a day and enjoy a calmer pace of life

Chapter 9

Making the most of your trip

Here are some advice on getting the most of your journey to Frankfurt:

Plan your schedule in advance
Frankfurt is a vast city, therefore it is vital to plan your itinerary in advance so that you can make the most of your time. Decide what you want to see and do, and then plan a timetable that will enable you to see everything you want.

Get a Frankfurt Card
The Frankfurt Card is a terrific way to save money on transit, sights, and excursions in Frankfurt. The card provides you free or subsidized entrance to over 60 attractions, as well as free public transit inside the city.

Walk around the city
Frankfurt is a relatively walkable city, so one of the greatest ways to explore is to just stroll about. This will offer you an opportunity to experience the city's many diverse areas, sights and features.

Take a boat cruise on the Main River

The Main River is an important stream that passes through Frankfurt. Taking a boat trip is a terrific chance to explore the city from a fresh perspective and learn about its history.

Visit the Goethe House
The Goethe House is the former residence of the German writer Johann Wolfgang von Goethe. It is now a museum that preserves Goethe's heritage and gives insights into his life and work.

Go shopping in the Zeil
The Zeil is a pedestrianized retail boulevard that is home to a number of high-end businesses. If you're wanting to do some shopping, make sure to check out the Zeil.

Try the local food
Frankfurt has a rich culinary past, so make sure to taste some of the local specialities. Some of the most popular meals are Frankfurter Würstchen, Äppler, Handkäs mit Musik, Grüne Soße, and Rindsrouladen.
Attend a cultural event
Frankfurt is a city with a bustling cultural life, so there is always something going on. Check out the local listings to discover what activities are occurring during your stay.

Relax at one of Frankfurt's numerous parks Frankfurt offers a lot of lovely parks, which are fantastic places to relax and enjoy the outdoors. Some of the more popular parks are the Palmengarten, the Botanischer Garten, and the Grüneburgpark.

Take a day excursion to adjacent cities

Frankfurt is situated in the middle of Germany, thus it is convenient to take day excursions to adjacent cities. Some of the most popular day trip locations are Heidelberg, Cologne, and Mainz.

Take advantage of SaTURday
Many of the largest museums in Frankfurt provide free admittance on the last Saturday of the month.

Get a transit day pass
If you don't want to buy the Frankfurt Card (which covers unlimited public transport), you may obtain a conventional transit day ticket. It costs 5.50 EUR, which is substantially less than paying each ride.

carry a water bottle – The tap water here is safe to drink so carry a reusable water bottle to save money and decrease your plastic consumption. LifeStraw is my go-to brand since its bottles have built-in filters to guarantee your water is always pure and safe.

Stay with a local — If you want to save money on accommodation while obtaining some insight from the locals, consider Couchsurfing. It's a terrific chance to meet people in the city and explore some off-the-beaten-path locations while also obtaining free lodging.

When to Go to Frankfurt
Summer is the major tourist season, notably July and August. The average daily temperatures are in the mid 20s°C (high 70s°F) and days are sunny and bright. You'll be rubbing shoulders with plenty of other visitors, but there are usually great festivals and activities going during this time.

Spring (April-May) and fall (October-November) are both shoulder seasons that provide lower weather, bright days, and less people. The best time to visit Frankfurt right now is if you want to take advantage of cheaper hotel rates and a more relaxed atmosphere!

Like the rest of Germany, Frankfurt's winters may be severe, with temperatures plunging below 1°C (34°F). The city sees occasional snowfall, but the Christmas markets during November and December are wonderful. It makes for a wonderful weekend vacation spot in the winter if you want to explore the Christmas markets.

Chapter 10

Staying Safe

Be mindful of your surroundings

Frankfurt is a secure city, however it is always vital to remain vigilant of your surroundings. This involves being aware of your things and avoiding going alone in dark locations at night.

Don't flash your valuables

If you are carrying valuables, such as a camera or a smartphone, take cautious not to flaunt them in public. This might make you a target for thieves.

Be cautious while utilizing ATMs

ATMs in Frankfurt are typically secure, however it is crucial to remain mindful of your surroundings while using one. If you are using an ATM in a public setting, make careful to stand in a well-lit area and be mindful of anybody who may be lurking nearby.

Don't consume too much alcohol

If you are going to be consuming alcohol, be sure to do it in moderation. Drinking too much alcohol might weaken your judgement and leave you more susceptible to crime.

Trust your intuition

If you feel uncomfortable in a situation, heed your instincts and leave. It is always better to be safe than sorry.

Here are some extra tips:

Stay informed about local events and alerts
The Frankfurt Tourist Board website gives up-to-date information about local events and advice.

Use a travel safety app
There are a variety of travel safety applications available that may offer you information about safety in various places. Some popular travel safety applications include:
TravelSafe App
TripAdvisor World Travel Guide

Learn some fundamental German phrases
Learning some simple German words will help you converse with locals and prevent misunderstandings.

Frankfurt Travel Guide 2023

Roy Writt

Printed in Great Britain
by Amazon